We Deliver It!

WE DRIVE
Dump Trucks

Ruby Tuesday Books

Alix Wood

Little Acorns

Published in 2026 by Ruby Tuesday Books Ltd.

Copyright © 2026 Ruby Tuesday Books Ltd.

All rights reserved. No part of this publication may be reproduced in whole or in part, stored in any retrieval system, or transmitted in any form or by any means, electronic, mechanical, photocopying, recording, or otherwise, without written permission from the publisher.

Editors: Ruth Owen & Mark J. Sachner
Design & Production: Alix Wood

Photo credits:
Alamy: 14B (Stephen Barnes/Transport), 16 (Ashley Cooper pics), 20 (Deborah Howe); iStockPhoto: 3 (Miguel Perfectti), 8B (LordHenriVoton), 9 (Andyqwe), 10T (Phynart Studio); Shutterstock: Cover (Mr. Tempter), 1 (igormakarov/Manop Boonpeng), 4 (Rob Wilson), 5 (MuchMania/WinWin artlab), 6 (aappp), 7T (Carolyn Franks), 7B (Olexa Misyachny), 8T (General Photographer), 10B (Tatiana Stulbo/Elena Istomina), 11 (Dmitry Kalinovsky), 12 (Deek), 13T (Darius Sul), 13B, 14T (Nerthuz), 15T (yanchi1984), 15B (Nerthuz), 17T (Alex Sobal), 17B (Tanes Ngamsom), 18 (M. Khebra), 19 (Miguel Perfectti), 21 (Maksim Safaniuk), 22T (Marius Dobilas), 22C (Another77), 22B (Rob Wilson), 23T (RobSt), 23C (RobSt), 23B (Vadim Ratnikov).

Library of Congress Control Number: 2024948697

Print (Hardback) ISBN 978-1-78856-525-7
Print (Paperback) ISBN 978-1-78856-526-4
ePub ISBN 978-1-78856-527-1

Published in Minneapolis, MN
Printed in the United States

www.rubytuesdaybooks.com

Contents

Moving Mountains 4

Glossary 22

Index 24

Moving Mountains

Many vehicles work at a **construction site**.

Dump trucks are big, powerful vehicles that can carry away unwanted soil.

Excavator

Dump truck

Dump trucks also collect construction materials, such as rock and sand, from **quarries**.

Then they deliver the materials to construction sites.

Dump trucks carry their load in a large container known as a **bed**.

Cab

Bed

Wheels

Dump trucks need big wheels and tires to help carry their heavy loads.

Some dump trucks have extra wheels.

Extra wheels

The driver can drop down the extra wheels when the bed has a heavy load.

Wheels up

Wheels down

7

Dump truck drivers usually start work early.

First, they check that the truck is safe to drive.

Then they check where they need to go.

This driver's first job is to deliver some sand.

She drives to the sand quarry to collect it.

At the quarry, an excavator driver is waiting.

Excavator

The dump truck driver backs up to the excavator.

An excavator driver beeps their horn when the dump truck is in the right spot.

Then the excavator starts to load the truck with sand.

Excavator

Sand

The driver takes the load to where it is needed.

They park, and then press a button in the cab.

A **ram** lifts the back of the truck up into the air.

Ram

Tailgate

Sand

The sand starts to pour from the **tailgate**.

Some dump trucks tip forward instead of backward.

Ram

Other trucks tip sideways.

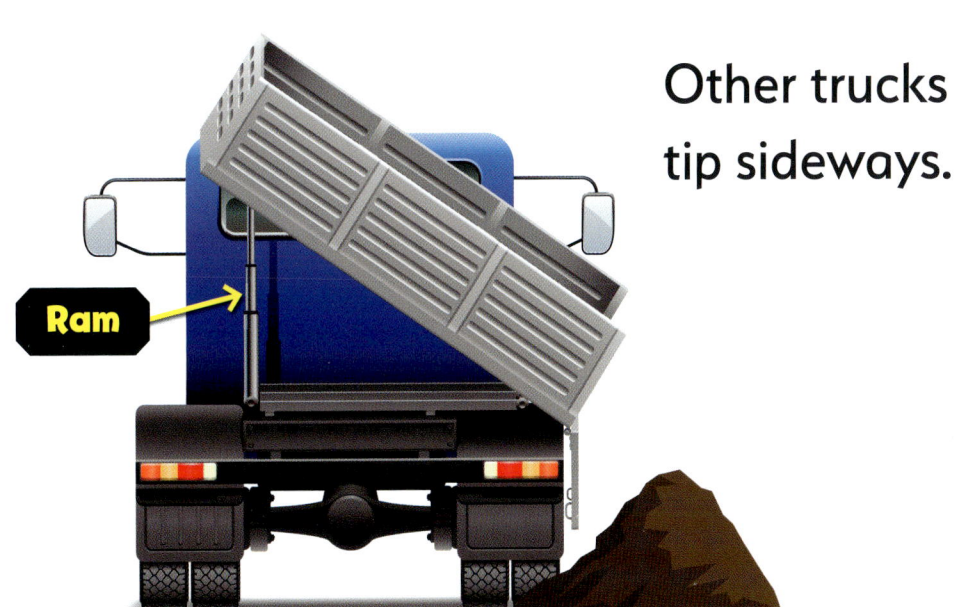

Ram

Some dump trucks are **articulated**.

The cab and the bed are joined by a hinge.

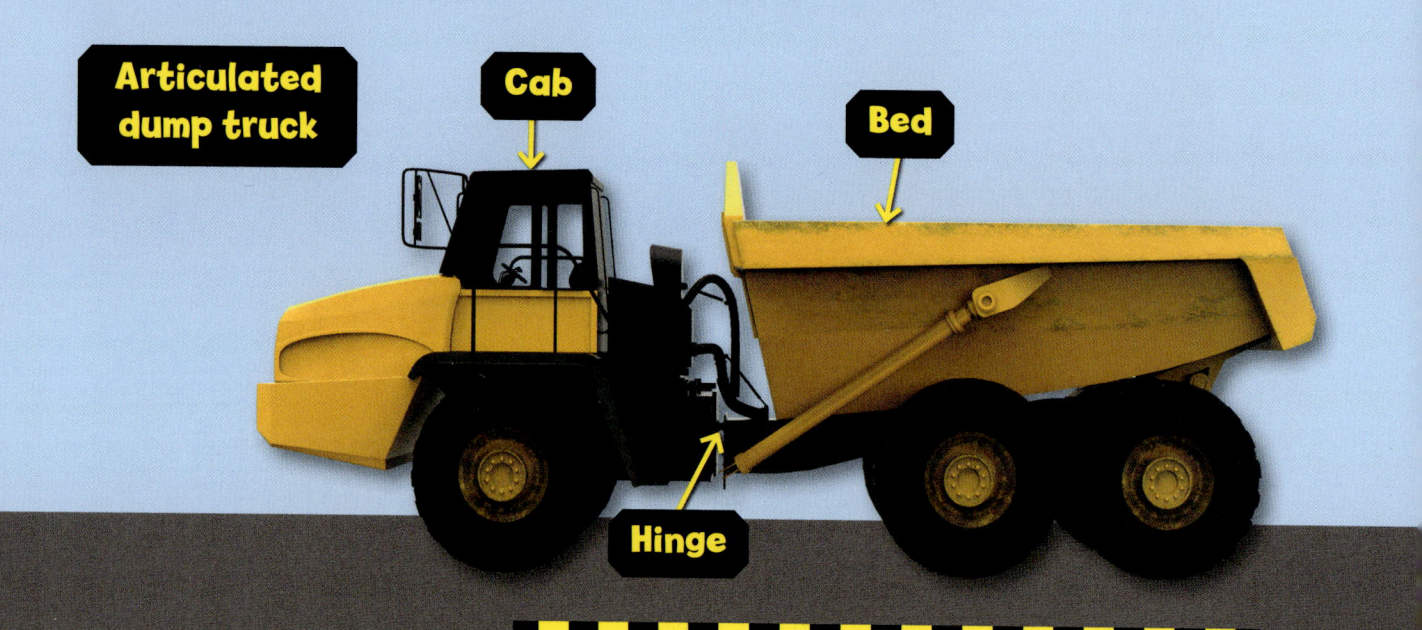

Articulated dump truck

Cab

Bed

Hinge

The hinge allows them to turn in small spaces.

On muddy or wet sites, drivers use dump trucks with tracks.

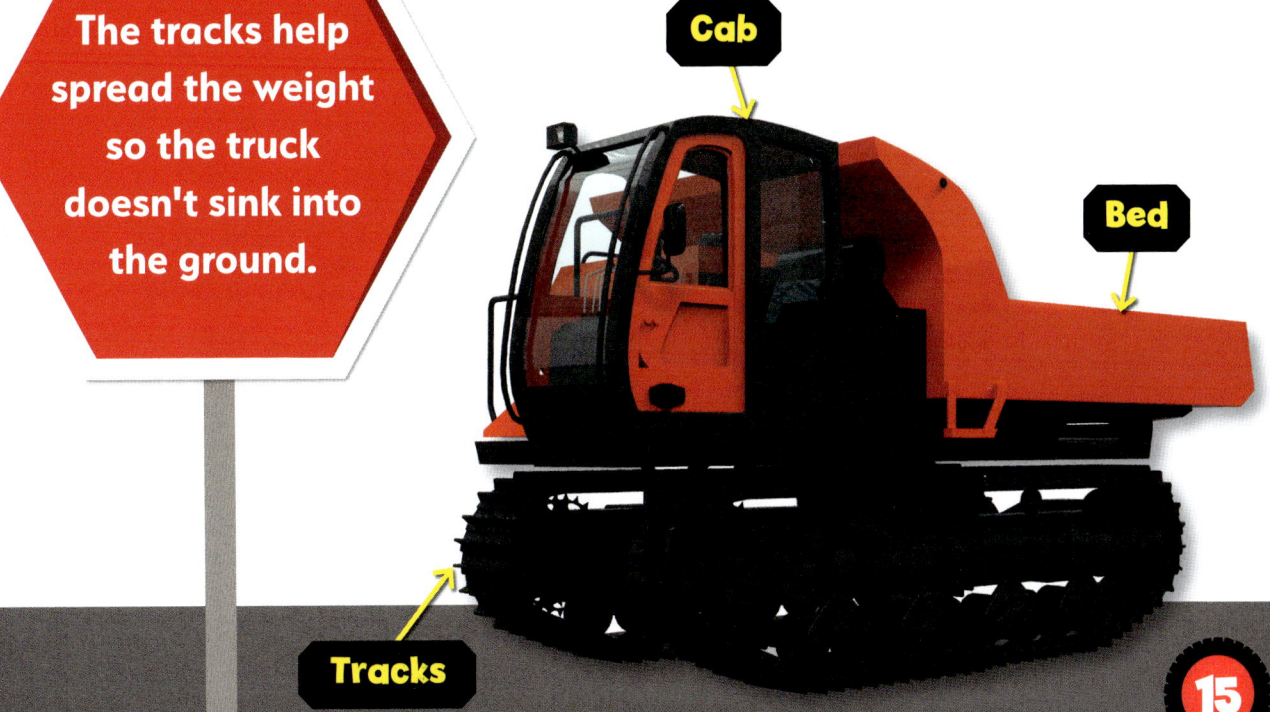

The tracks help spread the weight so the truck doesn't sink into the ground.

Cab

Bed

Tracks

To move very large loads, drivers use a giant dump truck.

These trucks are too big and heavy to drive on the road.

Giant dump trucks have to be carried to a site by a big, powerful truck.

This is the largest dump truck in the world.

The bed can carry the weight of three houses!

It has two engines.

Each wheel is taller than two people.

Giant dump trucks are so tall the driver climbs a ladder up to the cab!

Giant dump trucks are used in quarries.

They can carry huge loads of rock.

Giant excavator

Quarry workers

Rock

Giant dump truck

A giant excavator loads the rock.

Drivers use their mirrors and a camera to help them see as they back up.

Drivers sometimes have to tip their load over the edge of a steep drop.

The camera is under here on the tailgate.

Mirrors

Steep drop

Skillful dump truck drivers can even make their own roads!

They slowly pour out gravel as they drive backward.

The wheels push the gravel into the ground.

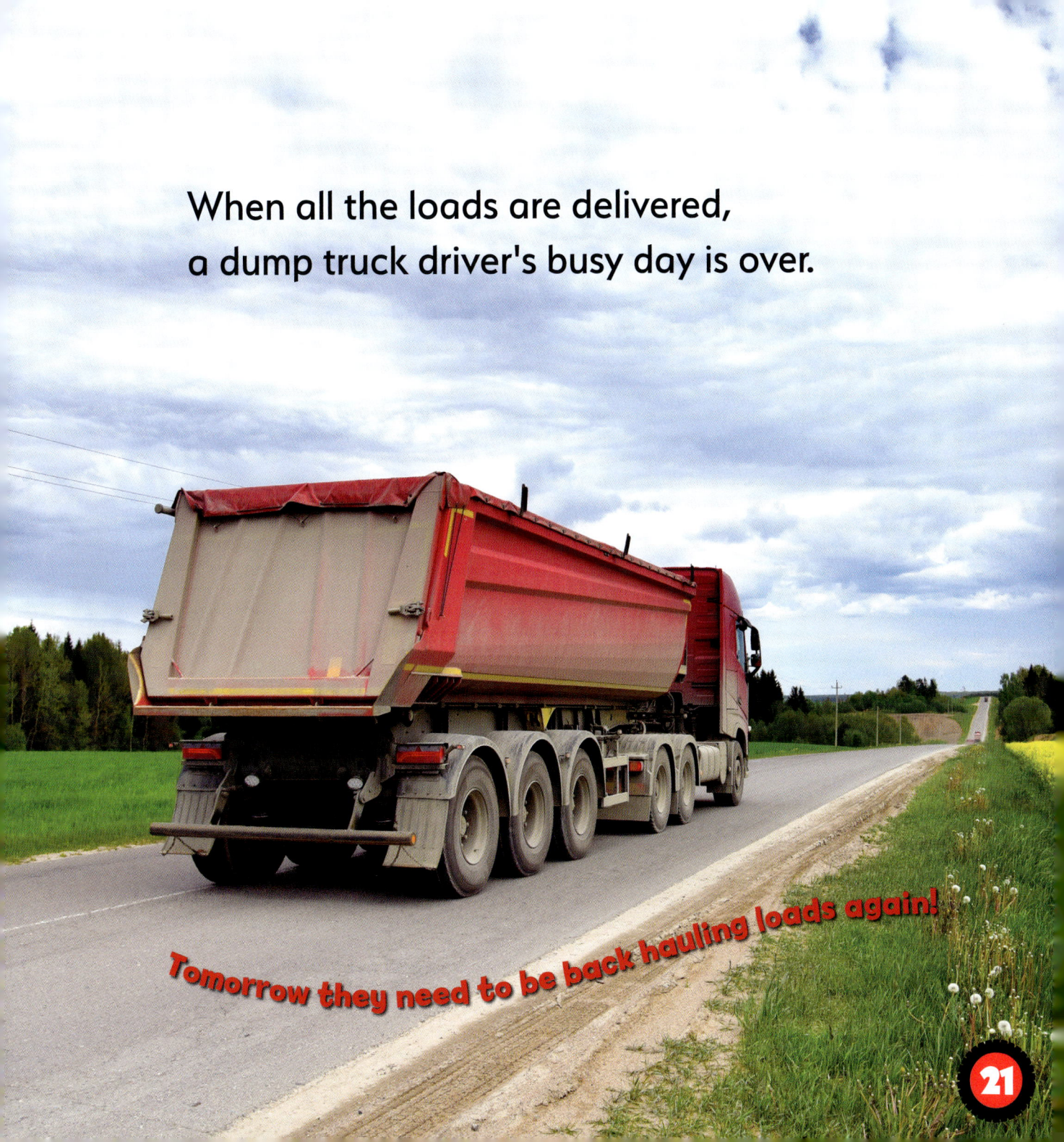

When all the loads are delivered,
a dump truck driver's busy day is over.

Tomorrow they need to be back hauling loads again!

Glossary

articulated
Having a hinge or joint that allows a vehicle to turn easily.

bed
The part of a dump truck that carries rock, sand, or other materials.

Bed

construction site
A piece of land where construction work is taking place.

quarry
A large hole in the ground from which rock or other materials are dug.

ram
A tube with a strong rod inside that can push the bed upward to dump a heavy load.

tailgate
A hinged panel or door on the back of a vehicle that can be opened to load or unload objects or materials.

Index

A
articulated dump trucks 14

B
beds 6–7, 14–15, 17

C
construction sites 4–5

E
excavators 4–5, 10–11, 18

G
giant dump trucks 16–17, 18

Q
quarries 5, 9, 10, 18

R
rams 12–13

T
tailgates 12, 19
tipping (a load) 12–13, 19
tracks 15

W
wheels 6–7, 17, 20